TABLETOP HOCKEY

Kids

Greg Peden

Kids Can Press

With all my love to Jeffrey, Emily and especially Lisa — G.P.

Text copyright © 2000 by Greg Peden
Photographs copyright © 2000 by Frank Baldassarra

All rights reserved. No part of this publication may be reproduced, stored in a retrieval system or transmitted, in any form or by any means, without the prior written permission of Kids Can Press Ltd. or, in case of photocopying or other reprographic copying, a license from CANCOPY (Canadian Copyright Licensing Agency), 1 Yonge Street, Suite 1900, Toronto, ON, M5E 1E5.

Many of the designations used by manufacturers and sellers to distinguish their products are claimed as trademarks. Where those designations appear in this book and Kids Can Press Ltd. was aware of a trade mark claim, the designations have been printed in initial capital letters (e.g., Top Corner Hockey).

Neither the Publisher nor the Author shall be liable for any damage which may be caused or sustained as a result of conducting any of the activities in this book without specifically following instructions, conducting the activities without proper supervision, or ignoring the cautions contained in the book.

Kids Can Press acknowledges the support of the Government of Canada, through the BPIDP, for our publishing activity.

Published in Canada by
Kids Can Press Ltd.
29 Birch Avenue
Toronto, ON M4V 1E2

Published in the U.S. by
Kids Can Press Ltd.
4500 Witmer Estates
Niagara Falls, NY 14305-1386

Edited by Elizabeth MacLeod
Designed by Julia Naimska
Technical design by Charlene Montgomery
Printed and bound in Canada

CM PA 00 0 9 8 7 6 5 4 3 2 1

Canadian Cataloguing in Publication Data
Peden, Greg
      Tabletop hockey : tips for kids

ISBN 1-55074-864-5

1. Tabletop hockey (game) — Juvenile literature.
2. Games for two — Juvenile literature.
I. Title.

GV1218.H57P42 2000   j794   C99-932830-1

Kids Can Press is a Nelvana company

Contents

Tabletop Hockey	4
The Story of the Game	6
Play Right	10
Shoot — Score!	12
Face-offs	14
How to Pass	16
Win with Your Wingers	18
Best Defense	20
Score with Your Defense	22
Great Goaltending	24
Practice Makes Perfect	26
Top Corner Hockey	28
Tournament Day	30

TABLETOP HOCKEY

Whether you call it tabletop hockey, rod hockey, knob hockey or flicker hockey, it is the same great game.

Kids have been playing tabletop hockey for more than 75 years. A few of those early games are now worth more than $20 000 each!

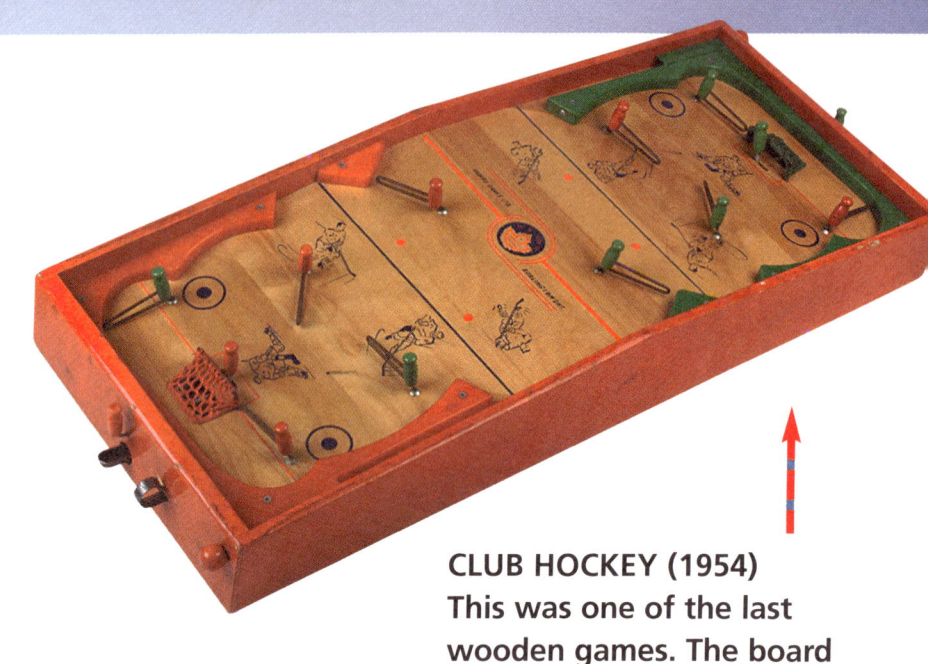

CLUB HOCKEY (1954)
This was one of the last wooden games. The board slopes down from the center toward each end.

Turn the page to see some of the most amazing hockey games ever.

Want to improve your play? It's easy if you follow the tips in this book. You'll discover how to win face-offs. You'll also find out how to defend your goal better. Plus you'll learn tricky plays to surprise your enemies.

Today there are millions of tabletop hockey players all over the world. Tournaments are held in many countries. Keep reading to find out what it is like to compete at one.

What's the most important thing to remember when playing tabletop hockey? Have fun!

5

THE STORY OF THE GAME

Tabletop hockey has changed a lot over the years. The game was invented in Canada over 75 years ago. You can see how it has changed in these photos.

HOCKEY-ETT (1923)
This was the first tabletop hockey game. The game's box turned into the rink. You used wire sticks to push the puck into the net. The game cost 85 cents in 1923 — today it is worth $5000.

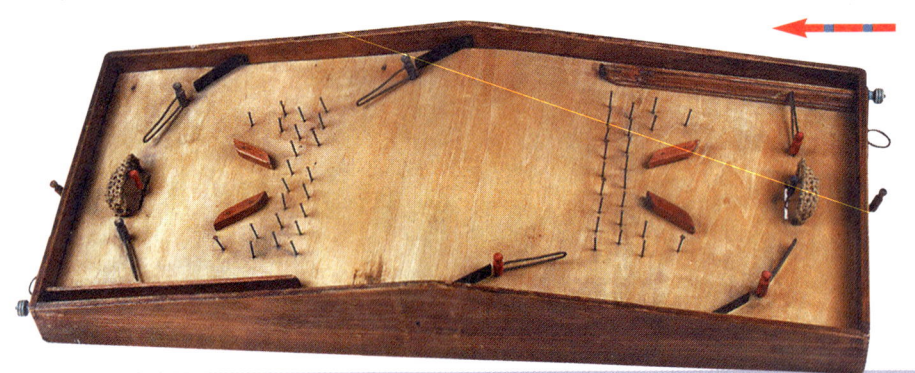

MUNRO (1936)
This game was the first that used levers to move the players. It was invented in the early 1930s. Rows of nails and blocks of wood were used instead of defensemen.

ICE HOCKEY (1937)
This was the first game made in the United States. Larger games like this could be found in arcades.

MAGNETIC HOCKEY (1940)
The players in this game were moved by powerful magnets held below the ice surface.

CRESTA (1954)
This was the first game to have tin players that moved along slots. The game was invented in Sweden in 1939.

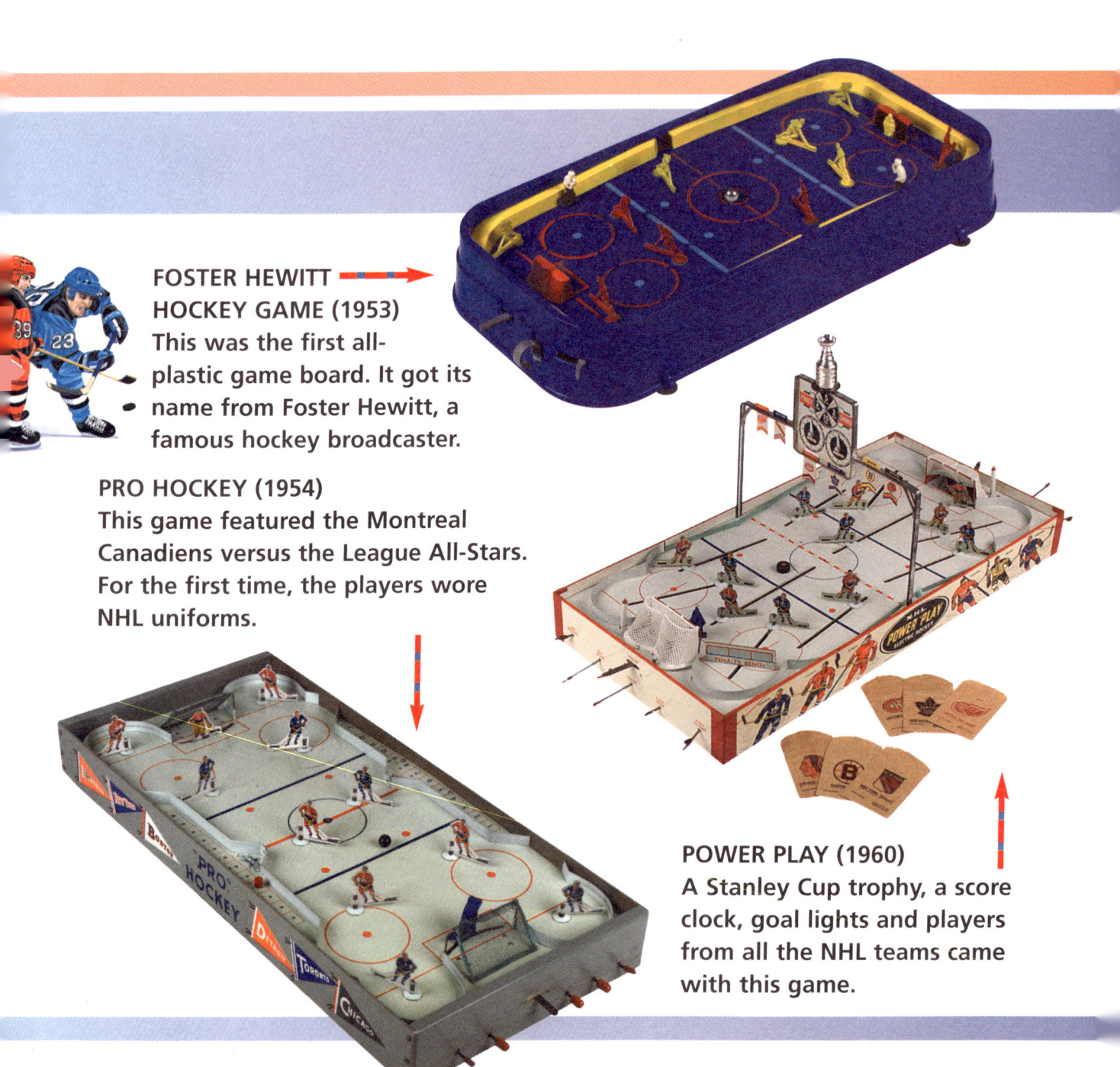

FOSTER HEWITT HOCKEY GAME (1953)
This was the first all-plastic game board. It got its name from Foster Hewitt, a famous hockey broadcaster.

PRO HOCKEY (1954)
This game featured the Montreal Canadiens versus the League All-Stars. For the first time, the players wore NHL uniforms.

POWER PLAY (1960)
A Stanley Cup trophy, a score clock, goal lights and players from all the NHL teams came with this game.

8

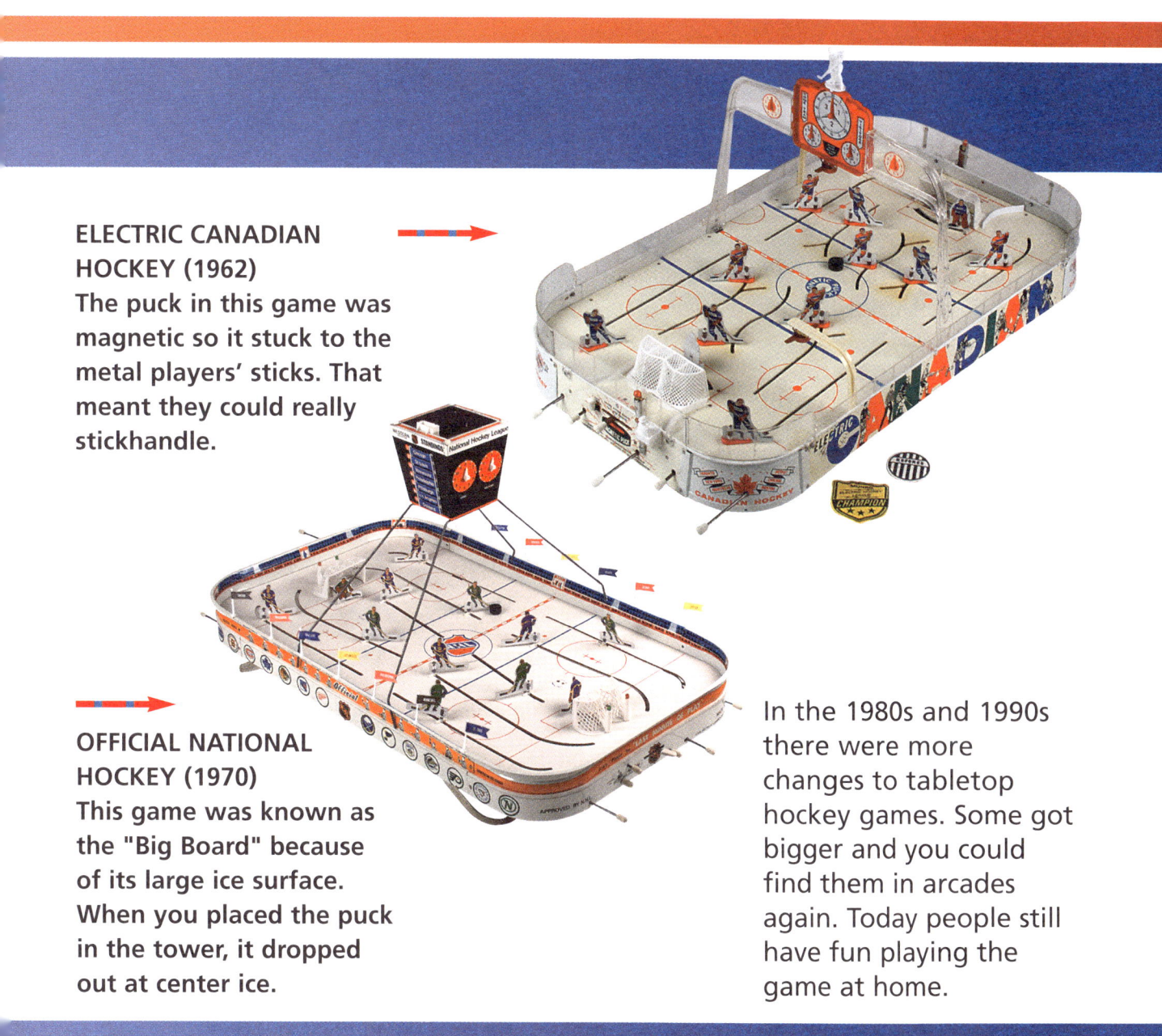

ELECTRIC CANADIAN HOCKEY (1962)
The puck in this game was magnetic so it stuck to the metal players' sticks. That meant they could really stickhandle.

OFFICIAL NATIONAL HOCKEY (1970)
This game was known as the "Big Board" because of its large ice surface. When you placed the puck in the tower, it dropped out at center ice.

In the 1980s and 1990s there were more changes to tabletop hockey games. Some got bigger and you could find them in arcades again. Today people still have fun playing the game at home.

Play Right

Here are some of the most important rules of tabletop hockey.

1. The referee is in charge of face-offs and calling penalties.

2. Games have three five-minute periods. Ties are decided by sudden-death overtime.

3. You have ten seconds to pass, shoot or clear the puck. If you don't, the puck is faced off at the nearest circle.

4. For a face-off, the puck is placed in the center of the face-off circle. Players' sticks must be outside the circle as shown below. They can only move when the referee calls "Go!" If the puck leaves the ice, players face off at the nearest circle.

5. A goal counts only if the puck stays in the net.

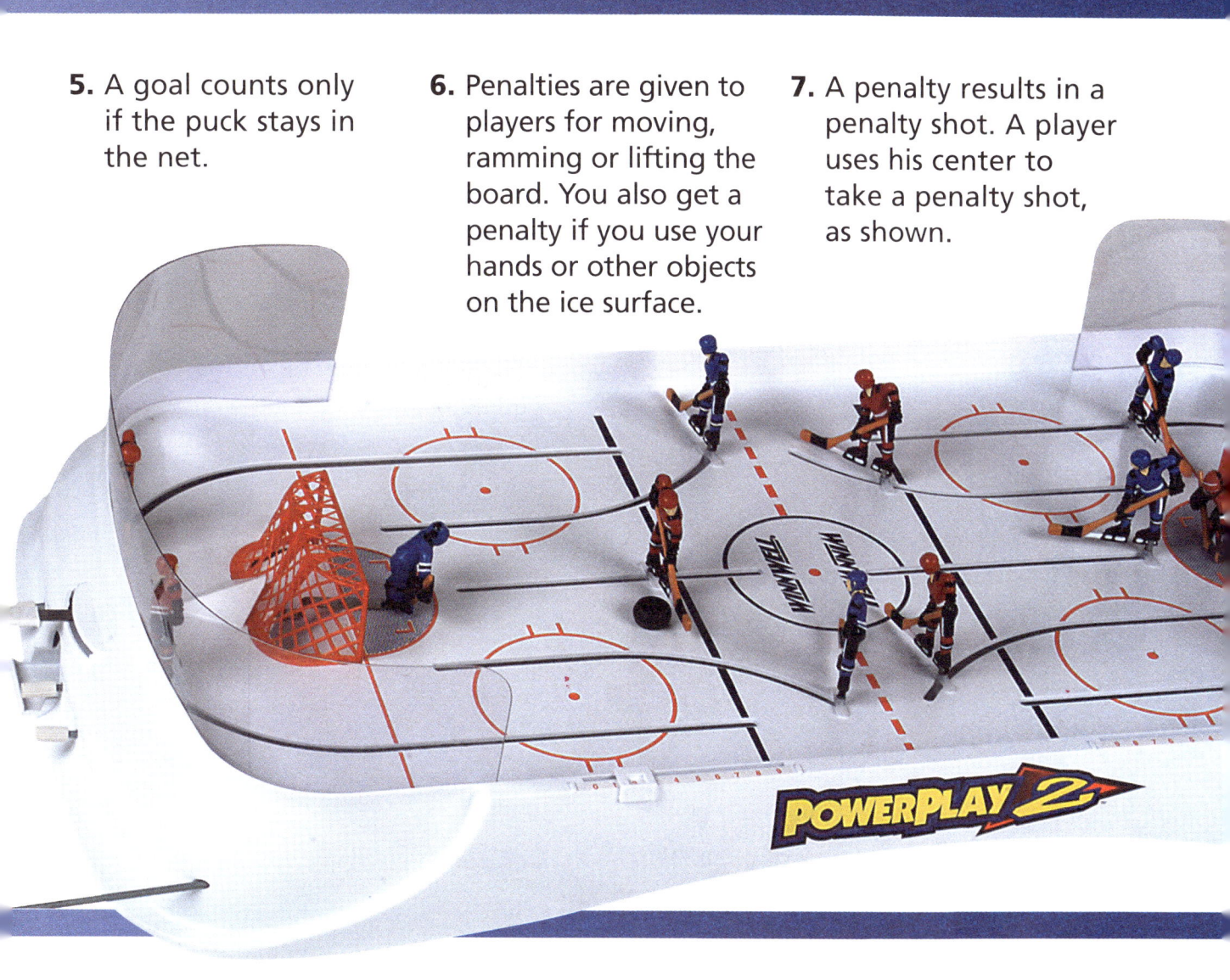

6. Penalties are given to players for moving, ramming or lifting the board. You also get a penalty if you use your hands or other objects on the ice surface.

7. A penalty results in a penalty shot. A player uses his center to take a penalty shot, as shown.

Shoot — score!

Your center is the most important part of your scoring attack.

When receiving passes, point your center's stick at the enemy goal. This will help you get a shot on net.

If you do not score, the puck may end up near the goal.

If this happens, move your center close to the goalie to pick up the rebound. Then spin him back and forth to knock the puck loose and get another shot on goal.

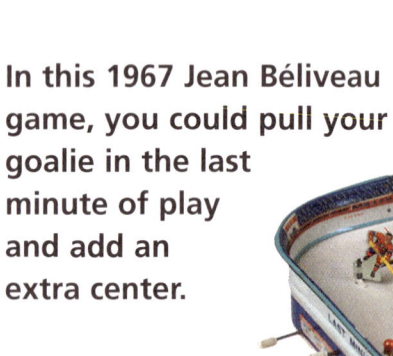

In this 1967 Jean Béliveau game, you could pull your goalie in the last minute of play and add an extra center.

Try surprising your enemy with the "center deke." There are three steps to this play, as shown.

1. Get the puck on your center's stick.

2. With a forehand or shooting motion, move the puck to the other side of your center's slot.

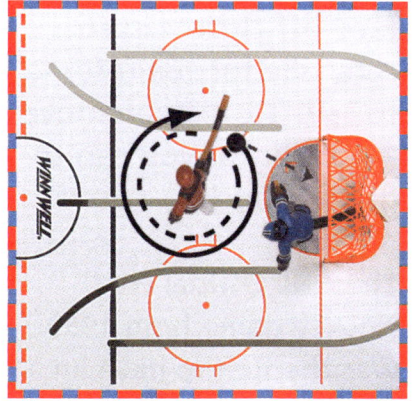

3. Spin around in a full circle away from the puck and shoot on net.

Face-offs

Winning face-offs will give your team the puck and a chance to score.

When taking face-offs, keep your player's stick out of the face-off circle. Listen carefully for the referee to say "Go!" Then move as quickly as you can to get the puck.

When you win face-offs at center ice, you can pass to either winger or fire a shot on goal.

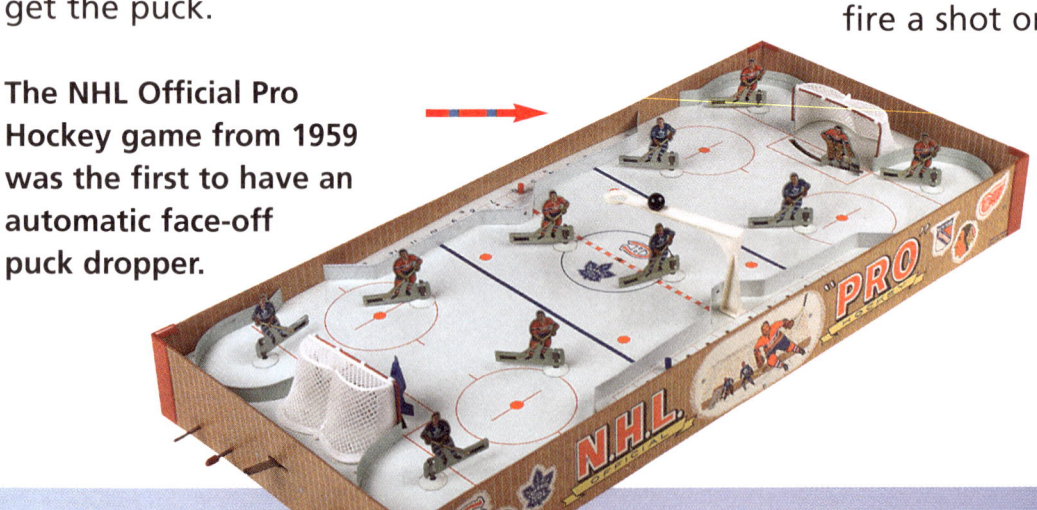

The NHL Official Pro Hockey game from 1959 was the first to have an automatic face-off puck dropper.

14

For face-offs in your end, keep your play simple. Win the draw and clear the puck out.

Expert Tip
Before all face-offs, position your goalie to stop a shot in case you lose the draw.

There are two plays your winger can make when the face-off is in your enemy's end. He can shoot the puck to the boards, pick it up there and set up a pass play. Or he can pass to the center for a shot on goal, as shown.

15

How to Pass

You will create your best scoring chances when you pass from your wingers to your center. When your winger has the puck, he cannot be checked. This gives you time to choose your next play.

What if your opponent puts one of his defensemen near his goalie? Pass to your center in front of the defenseman, as shown. After you take a shot on net, slide your center down to the enemy goal to grab the rebound.

Expert Tip

Fake a pass from your winger to center, then take a shot.

Pass from the stick blade, with the puck flat.

Sometimes your opponent will place his defenseman near his blue line. Move your winger past him and pass to your center for a tip-in play, as shown.

The National Hockey Electric game (1957) was the first with goal lights that lit up.

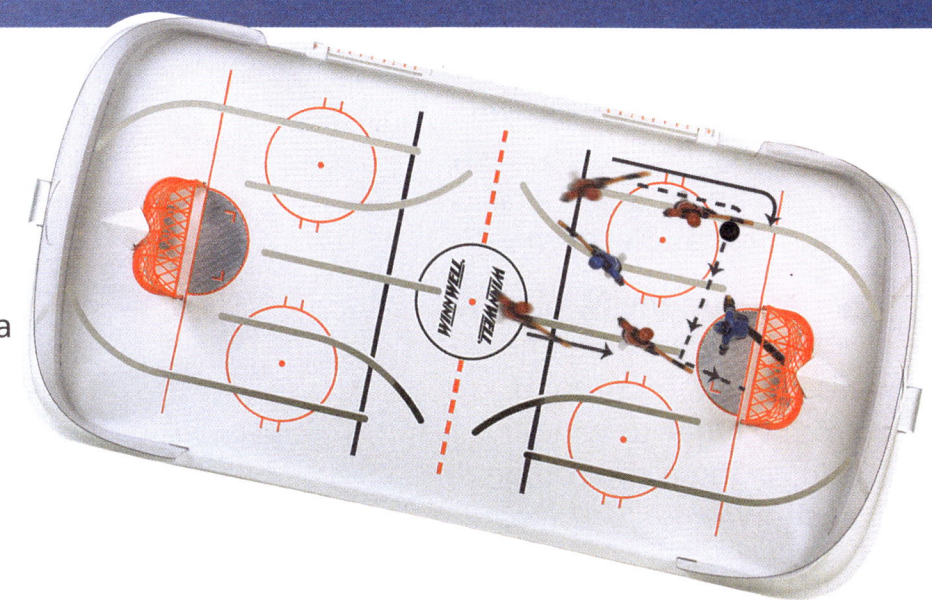

Expert Tip
Distract your opponent by sliding your center up and down his slot.

Win with your wingers

Your wingers are your best playmakers. They can pass, shoot and stickhandle.

Is your enemy playing his defensemen near his goalie? Try passing from winger to winger and taking a shot on goal, as shown.

Surprise your enemy by passing the puck from winger to winger behind his net. The winger receiving the pass should be at the face-off circle, as shown. When the puck reaches him, he can either take a shot or pass to his center.

18

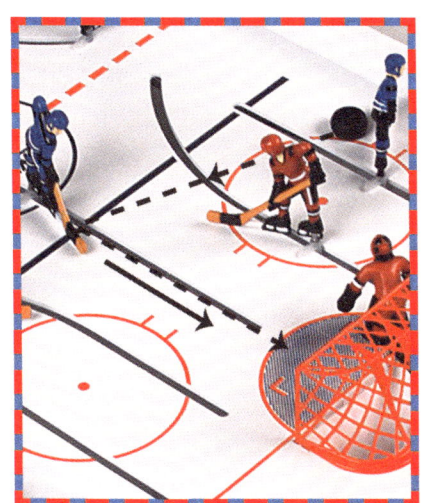

A great winger play is the "spin pass." Move your winger to the face-off circle. Keep the puck between the boards and your winger's slot. Make a backhand pass to your center (left), or spin and take a shot on goal (right). If you shoot, slide your center down to the net for a tip-in (below).

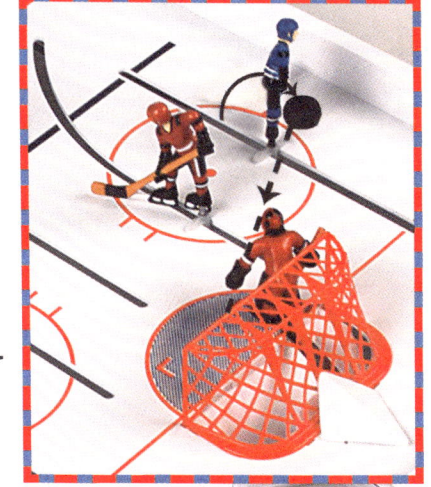

Expert Tip
When your winger takes a shot on goal, move your center close to the enemy net. That makes him ready for rebounds.

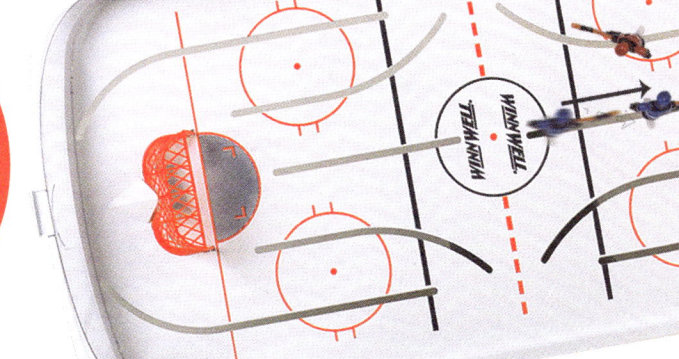

Best Defense

Smart defense helps keep the puck out of your net. Your defenseman's job is to block shots, cut off passes and also clear the puck.

When an enemy winger has the puck, look where he places it on his stick. If the puck is on the tip of his stick, he may be ready to shoot. Pull your defenseman back between the winger and your goalie to block the shot, as shown.

Expert Tip
Keep it simple when clearing the puck. It is better to shoot than to stickhandle too much.

If your opponent puts the puck at the heel of his stick, he might pass to his center. Slide your defenseman between the winger and center to cut off the pass, as shown.

Spinning or twirling your defenseman is dangerous. You might shoot the puck into your own net.

Expert Tip
Place each defensemen so that his stick points at the other team's goal. This lets you clear the puck better.

Score with your defense

Surprise your enemy by taking shots with your defensemen.

For the "jam shot," position the puck on the slot in front of your defenseman, as shown. Push or jam the puck with the base of your defenseman for a shot on goal.

When one of your defensemen has the puck, pass to the other one. Let him shoot on net, as shown. Use your center to pick up any rebounds in front of the enemy net.

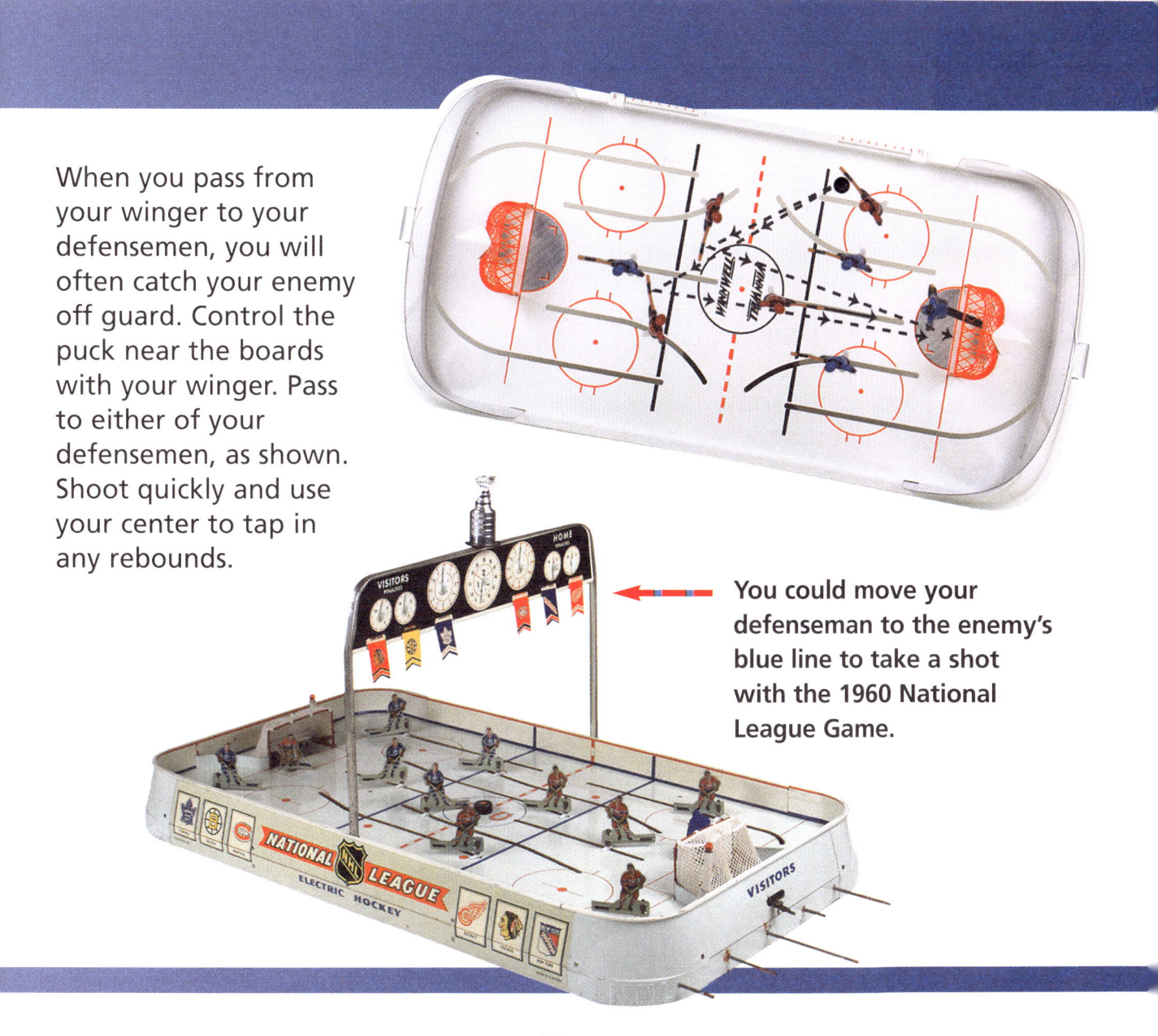

When you pass from your winger to your defensemen, you will often catch your enemy off guard. Control the puck near the boards with your winger. Pass to either of your defensemen, as shown. Shoot quickly and use your center to tap in any rebounds.

You could move your defenseman to the enemy's blue line to take a shot with the 1960 National League Game.

Great Goaltending

Great goaltending is a big part of winning tabletop hockey games.

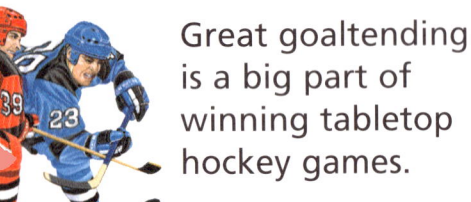

You can move your goalie across the crease to block shots. You can also push him out to cut down a shooter's angle or clear the puck.

When play is in your end, always keep one hand on your goalie. If enemy wingers have the puck, hold your goalie just less than one puck-width from the goalpost, as shown. This lets you stop far-side shots. You are also in a better place to cover passes to the center.

When your enemy's center has a breakaway, push your goalie out to the top of the crease to cut down the angle.

Expert Tip
When you are on the attack, center your goalie in his net. Then he is ready to stop any shot.

If the center moves toward your goalie to deke, pull your goalie back to the goal line, as shown. That stops the enemy from stickhandling around your netminder.

Practice Makes Perfect

To become a great tabletop hockey player, practice the plays you have learned in this book.

The most important play to practice is passing from your wingers to your center. Practice this pass from as many different spots as possible. This will help you score more goals.

Try the "full-team passing" drill. Pass to as many players as you can before you lose the puck (see below). Keep count of your passes, and try to beat your score next time!

If you are on your own, tape one goalie in the center of his net. Throw a few pucks on the ice, and then practice passing and shooting. Stop playing only when all the pucks are in the net.

With a friend, have a breakaway shootout. Each player gets five shots with his center. The player with the most goals wins!

Play the "no goalie" game. Remove the goalies and play a five-goal game with a friend.

Pee Wee hockey from 1956 was about half the size of a regular game. Younger players liked practicing on it.

Top Corner Hockey

Tabletop hockey changed a lot when Top Corner Hockey was created in 1993.

Top Corner players can twist at their waists and take slapshots. They can raise the puck. That means they can shoot at the top corners of the enemy's net.

Use the pump-action control on the rods to do this.

The Top Corner goalie is different from other netminders. He can move his blocker arm to stop shots. He can also poke out his stick to clear the puck.

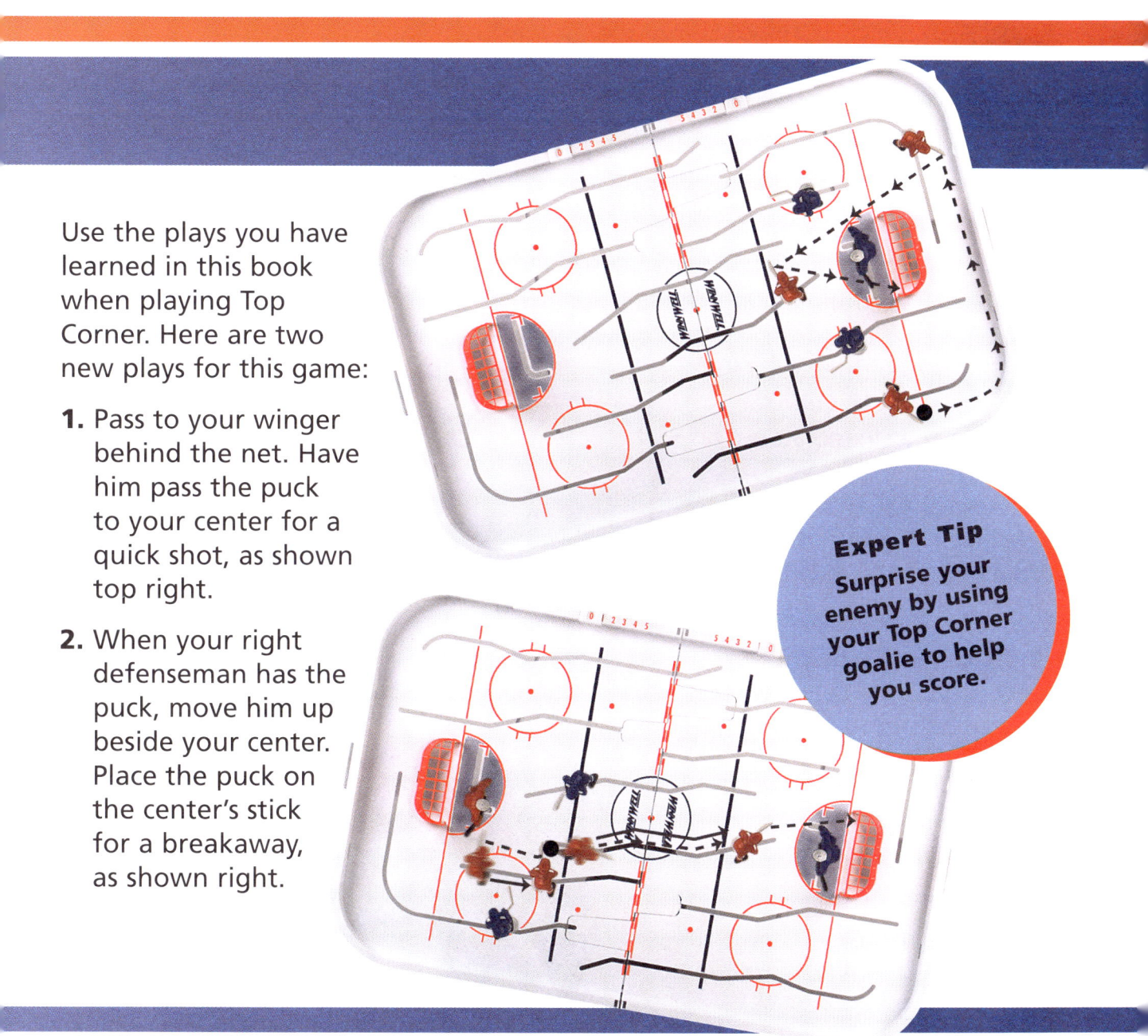

Use the plays you have learned in this book when playing Top Corner. Here are two new plays for this game:

1. Pass to your winger behind the net. Have him pass the puck to your center for a quick shot, as shown top right.

2. When your right defenseman has the puck, move him up beside your center. Place the puck on the center's stick for a breakaway, as shown right.

Expert Tip
Surprise your enemy by using your Top Corner goalie to help you score.

Tournament Day

The Upper Canada Irwin Cup tabletop hockey tournament is very exciting. More than 70 of the best players from Canada and the United States compete. In the finals, the top Canadian meets the best U.S. player. Here's what it is like to play in that tournament.

7:00 A.M. I pull on my Toronto Maple Leaf sweater for good luck. I pack a sandwich for lunch and bring plenty of water.

9:00 A.M. I arrive at the tournament and register. Then I study the rules for the tournament carefully.

9:30 A.M. Play begins. I play well in the early rounds. This is important because the games are short and you can get knocked out easily.

3:00 P.M. I have not lost a game all day. In between matches, I watch other players. I want to see who is winning and what plays they are using. If I play them later, I will be prepared.

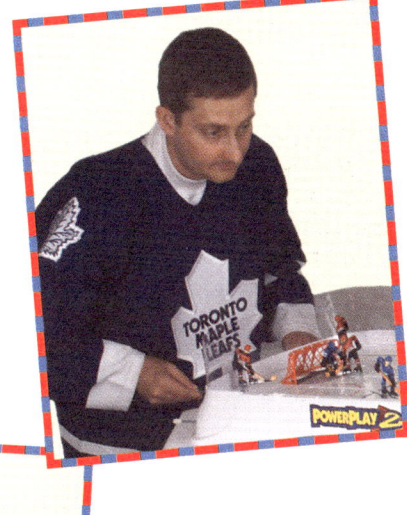

7:00 P.M. I make it to the finals! I will be playing for Canada against the best U.S. player. My opponent is tough. The games are close and I have to use all the plays I know. Finally I win the championship, four games to two.

8:30 P.M. I am presented with the Irwin Cup and $1000. This is a day I will always remember.

Expert Tip
If you are knocked out of tournament play, learn from your mistakes so you can be better next time.